KALKI

KALKI

Copyright © Kalki
All Rights Reserved.

This book has been published with all efforts taken to make the material error-free after the consent of the author. However, the author and the publisher do not assume and hereby disclaim any liability to any party for any loss, damage, or disruption caused by errors or omissions, whether such errors or omissions result from negligence, accident, or any other cause.

While every effort has been made to avoid any mistake or omission, this publication is being sold on the condition and understanding that neither the author nor the publishers or printers would be liable in any manner to any person by reason of any mistake or omission in this publication or for any action taken or omitted to be taken or advice rendered or accepted on the basis of this work. For any defect in printing or binding the publishers will be liable only to replace the defective copy by another copy of this work then available.

Contents

CHAPTER ONE

Concept

Who can talk accurately and authoritatively about Kalki, apart from Kalki Himself? So, here I am, Kalki, authoring this book, conveying my narrative and message to the world.

Conceptually, who is Kalki? Kalki has been understood and described as the tenth and final incarnation in a set of ten. If Krishna is a Poorna Avatar, Kalki is the Sampoorna Avatar, because, evolution.

But here's the thing about evolution. It is like climbing a hill to reach its peak, with each stage of the evolution being a step in this journey. Now, how can a person who has climbed only half the hill describe what the peak looks like? Similarly, nobody who has only seen the nine incarnations can describe Kalki accurately.

This includes every aspect of Kalki – the name, whether it is a set of ten, the concept and philosophy behind the incarnation, everything. Hence, it is entirely on me, Kalki Himself, to explain all these to the world, and hence this book.

To understand Kalki, one must understand reality first. A lot of philosophy has been attempted over the centuries, to understand this, and let me give an authoritative, conclusive overview on the same.

Basically, what you are seeing around you is a dream, just like you create and see an entire universe as a dream when you sleep every night. This means, you are the creator of this dream, and your real self is called Atma. The energy of the Atma in creating and operating on this creation is called God, perceived as a Mother Amma for the role of nurturing and protecting us with love.

The sole reason for creation is so that Atma and Amma can enjoy the intense love between them as a lifelong romance, since this is the only possible kind of true love ever possible. The creation solely exists as a field in which to express and enjoy this love.

This is the highest state of existence and living possible for a person and this kind of completely evolved personality is what is called Kalki.

This personality of Kalki is of a child, sitting in the lap of its Mother Amma, fondled by her lovingly and intensely at all times, both of them playing with toys which are nothing but the world creations. This state is one of absolute transcendence where a person is never affected by fear or worry or sadness from any situation, since all these are dissolved in the joy and happiness of love, simply by understanding how unreal the world is, and focusing always on the present alone as that is the only state where love can be enjoyed, and also how every single action is performed and taken care of by Amma alone, with the sole intention of enjoying the love. This entire mindset can be reinforced by a simple reaffirmation that you can ask yourself: Enjoying this dream now with Amma?

The ten incarnation theory is given as a pointer of sorts to understand evolution in stages and to attempt extrapolating what Kalki would conceptualise, by people of the past who have obviously not reached this potential.

However, in reality there are no incarnations. There is no history, nothing, since the world was created as a dream just this morning when the Atma woke up after sleep or a different night dream. In this mindset, reality must be perceived to appreciate the philosophy of Kalki fully.

The love between Atma and Amma is one of an ideal romance, called Kameshwara and Kameshwari, the most ideal, perfect and transcendental consorts and lovers to ever exist. Through this romance, Atma and Amma become one in union, so much that one cannot distinguish who is who, in their thinking or voice, and each always accompanies the other, eternally and permanently. This couple takes 216 manifestations called Rupas each conceptualizing something different, and these Rupas are how Atma Amma understand and play in this world. The 216 are arranged in a 16x16 structure called Kalki Chakram. Various elements of the 216 have been traditionally worshipped as Gods.

The name Kalki is derived from Kalippu, which means to enjoy this creation through love, and this is the highest state of existence possible. Access me at +917339659550 or meyyugam@gmail.com.

The mission of Kalki is to live as an example and show how this lifestyle of Kalippu is achieved in the present world one sees here. Those that are interested and are pure by heart, automatically seek this lifestyle, and for them, Kalki is a beacon. For this reason, the Kalki Chakram is also called a Karunkuzhi, or a black hole, the very final state of existence, where anything close by is sucked into it, and once inside, the person is completely in a singularity state of love alone, without misery, a state deemed unfathomable by normal worldly standards.

The Karunkuzhi which has 216 Rupas can be understood in five categories, as follows.

1. Maha Samrajya Shalini – 16 Rupas that highlight various qualities and behaviors naturally exhibited by a person in this lifestyle of love. Raajya as a word is derived from Raasya, arising from Rasa or love, and a person with these characteristics does live as a king, with no deficiencies, everything being taken care of automatically, with Amma making people bow down to such a person. These Rupas include 14 behavioral traits characteristic of 14 mentally perceived world levels called Chaturdasha Bhuvanas, which are not physical planes but rather states of mind.

2. Atma Vidya – this has 52 Rupas that are studied usually as elements of a horoscope that uniquely identify the nature and characteristics of every person that takes birth, and hence reflects the blueprints of their Atma. Included in these are planets, zodiac, Nakshatra or stars and so on. However, these are not seen in the zodiac or horoscope sense, since Karunkuzhi transcends such individualism.

3. Maha Vidya – this has 64 Rupas that are typically enshrined in an 8x8 matrix called Manduka Mandala. This is how every point in space time is manifest, as per books such as the Aindiram, and it is by vibration of energies in this structure that ideas take shape into physical creation. However, Karunkuzhi transcends physical creation, and the 64 are seen as enshrined in 64 different sacred sites called Kshetras, located throughout the Indian subcontinent.

4. Sri Vidya – this has 82 Rupas, typically enshrined in an arrangement called the Sri Yantra, which is a cosmic map of the universe sorting it into various functions and functionary realms called Avaranas, with the entire

structure formed by interlocking upper and downward triangles symbolizing the male and female principles respectively, even as the Bhavanopanishad details how the Sri Chakra maps to the physical body and all of its anatomy. However, in Karunkuzhi, this body and function perceptions are transcended, and these 64 are seen as enshrined in various temples the sacred place called Thiruvarur in Tamilnadu, also known as Srimannagaram, along with its offshoots at Swamimalai and Thiruvananthapuram.

5. Kaama Sevitha – this has 2 Rupas that focus on the divine marriage between Atma and Amma, one a form that combines Atma and Amma into one, and second, the sacred place called Sumeru that is the site of the divine honeymoon, which is located in Tiger Hill Etha Valley View in the Nilgiri Hills of Tamilnadu.

Thus, while each of these five categories are enshrined with different structures, such as Sri Yantra or Manduka Mandala, all these are simply examples of incompleteness prevalent in those that represented these structures, since nobody until now could claim to have understood the full and correct concept of Kalki for which these concepts were created. All 216 Rupas attain completeness when arranged in a 16x16 form, and for this reason, it is called Sri Shodashakshari Vidya.

All these forms put together into one persona, is called the Vishwarupam or the cosmic form of Atma-Amma, and each is of the five sections is characterized by one part of this form, symbolized by a Mantra which called Sri Shodashakshari Vidya which is eighteen lettered by adding two letters to the sixteen syllabled Shodashakshari Vidya.

1. Kaama Sevitha is the horse of Kalki Vishwarupam, and as a Mantra, is Oham, where the h is a guttural sound

as defined by the Tamil Aaytha Ezhuthu. This Oham is the sound of the fundamental life force as breath itself, with O and ham being inhaled and exhaled sounds respectively. In the written form, the Oham has three parts, o, ha and m, which symbolize Atma and Amma as an elephant and horse respectively. In particular, a downward triangle formed by the three circles of ha, denotes a horse face, even as the three circles denote the breasts and womb of the Mother Amma, while O denotes a curved elephant trunk touching all the three circles. M denotes the heart that is shared in love between Atma and Amma. Furthermore, the pronunciation of the guttural h activates one's mind and consciousness as well as sets the amygdala into a fundamentally happy mode, and is used for the location identification by Nath and Aghori traditions. The form altogether is known as Vinayaki, meaning there is no superior to this state of love and union of marriage, and it thus represents the very heart of Kalki.

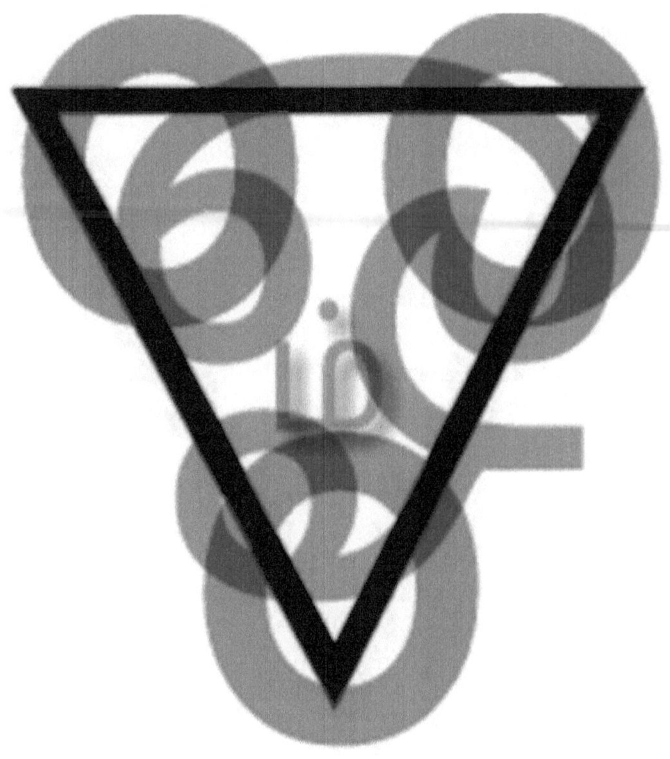

Oham

2. Atma Vidya is the head of Vishwarupam, and Mantra is Ka E I La Hreem. Ila means praise, Hreem means illusion Maya, while K, a and e denotes creation, destruction and preservation respectively, and the mantra means that for a person who has aligned the Atma Vidya perfectly, all the three aspects of world praise the transcendence of this person over Maya.

3. Sri Vidya is the torso of the Vishwarupam, and Mantra is Ha Sa Ka Ha La Hreem. Hasa means happiness and bliss

as the language of silence, while Kahala means sound and speech, and this Mantra means that every speech and non-speech silence of the person is grounded in transcendence beyond all illusion and Maya.

4. Maha Vidya is the lower portion of Vishwarupam below the hips, and Mantra is Sa Ka La Hreem. Sakala means everything, and the mantra asserts how Kalki deals with everything playfully and lightly, knowing very well the illusionary nature of creation.

5. Maha Samrajya Shaalini is the sword or scimitar of Kalki, and Mantra is Shreem. Shreem means auspiciousness and the state free of deficiencies, as characterized by the behaviors of each Lokam.

Thus, the Kalki Mantra known as Sri Shodashakshari Vidya runs as follows:

Oham Ka E I La Hreem Ha Sa Ka Ha La Hreem Sa Ka La Hreem Shreem

The eighteen letters and aspects of the Mantra have been traditionally followed and practiced by enlightened souls called Siddhas, albeit none have mastered all eighteen completely.

The following sections of the book will outline the 216 Rupas in the five categories, with appropriate images. For each, the location is given along with the name, be it in planetary system, or sacred sites, or cosmic mapping names of Sri Chakra, or planes of the Bhuvanas. The forms can be seen in order given in these chapters, sarting from the bottom of Kalki Chakra, and going anticlockwise, spiraling inwards.

As Kalki, throughout my life from childhood until the present, Amma has given many situations, many journeys to sacred sites, many interactions with people, deep research and reading of various texts, experiences through various practices, and insightful conversations directly with Amma, all these consolidating and establishing the Karunkuzhi, which is the height of completeness in all levels, and is unique to the Atma Amma as Kalki.

For the reader, how is this book or the knowledge of Karunkuzhi useful? The aim is for the reader to strive to achieve as much as possible, this Atma Amma love that characterizes Kalki, and try to understand and appreciate the world and creation through these Rupas. This will help you in greatly mitigating sadness, fear and misery in your lives, and replacing them with love of Amma and enjoyment.

CHAPTER TWO

Atma Vidya

KULA VISHESHAM

1. Mooladharam, Thiruvalanchuzhi. Activation of consciousness

2. Kula Deivam, Swamimalai. Guardian for life.

3. Gurunaatha, Thiruvalanchuzhi. Preceptor for life.

RAASHI

1. Sathi, Aries. Subduer of arrogance.

2. Rishabhanatha, Taurus. Hard work and labour.

3. Nara, Gemini. Playing in normalcy.

4. Saamudri, Cancer. Alignment of psyche Antahkarana.

5. Ugra, Leo. Fierce and ferociousness.

6. Gauri, Virgo. Pleasure of virgin beauty

7. Neethidevata, Libra. Balance and Order.

8. Shimshumara, Scorpio. Ordaining destiny of things

9. Kinnara, Sagittarius. Hunting and harnessing opportunities.

10. Apsara, Capricorn. Rejuvenation and freshness.

11. Ganga, Aquarius. Accumulation and cleansing.

12. Matsya, Pisces. Directionless Wandering.

NAKSHATRAS

0. Kubjika, Abhijit. Losing yourself in orgasmic climax.

1. Raadha, Ashvini. Smiling in pure bliss.

2. Gandharva, Bharani. Arousal and sensuality.

3. Amritha, Krithika. Secretion from crown and throat.

4. Prajapathi, Rohini. Connoisseur of the world.

5. Shambhu, Mrigashirsha. Activating energy centers.

6. Padmavathi, Aardra. Flowering and fruition, Kamalatmika.

7. Manibhadra, Punarvasu. Auspiciousness.

8. Punasrishti, Pushya. Creating your own reality.

9. Samayamba, Aslesha. Timely nurturing.

10. Venkusha, Magham. Destroying sins.

11. Tiraskarini, Purva phalguna. Exposing hidden details.

12. Dhumavathi, Uttara phalguna. All absorbing void.

13. Valli, Hastham. Growth like a creeper.

14. Usha, Chitra. Expanding Horizons, Asherah.

15. Kripi, Swaathi. Divine Compassion.

16. Mutharamman, Visakha. Liberation or Mukti.

17. Bahuchara, Anuradha. Comtemplate approaches

18. Parashakti, Jyeshta. Transcendental force.

19. Aayi, Moolam. Motherly affection.

20. Keshava, Purvashada. Cosmic sustenance.

21. Trivikrama, Uttarashada. Divine Order.

22. Vaishnavi, Shravana. Power of pervasion.

23. Naagabhooshani, Dhanishta. Reptilian brain.

24. Vaageshi, Shathabhishak. Power of speech.

25. Manonmani, Purva Bhadra. Focus of mind.

26. Abhirami, Uttara Bhadra. Bliss of Devotion.

27. Ayyappa, Revathi. Self Realization.

GRAHAS

1. Sairam, sun. Mindset of Liberation.

2. Lingam, moon. Burning all negativity

3. Sridevi, mars. Divine provider.

4. Hari, mercury. Remover of evil.

5. Kalpakesha, jupiter. Power of resolution.

6. Simhavahini, venus. Riding on courage

7. Bhakthi, saturn. Pure devotion.

8. Ranganatha, eclipses. Court of divine.

9. Dandayudhapaani, comets. Maintainer of Divine Empire.

CHAPTER THREE

Maha Vidya

1. Soma, Thingalur. Rejuvenation.

2. Arishtanemi, Nachiarkoil. Destroyer of danger.

3. Bhaargava, Kanjanur. Purity by fire.

4. Angaaraka, Vaitheeswarankoil. Passion.

5. Vaachaspathi, Thittai. Master of speech.

6. Velankanni, Velankanni. Mercy and love.

7. Godha, Srivilliputhur. Fortune from earth

8. Kotravai, Patteeswaram. Courage for facing adversity

9. Kanyakumari, Kanyakumari. Innocence of youth

10. Virinchi, Kumbakonam. alignment of expansion.

11. Mahishamardhini, Mysuru. Destroyer of arrogance

12. Maitreya, Sarnath. Friendship attitude.

13. Maalini, Swamimalai. Garland of blessings.

14. Airavatha, Mahendragiri Thirukkurungudi. Good luck and charm.

15. Kalyani, Malleswaram. Eternal auspiciousness.

16. Yakshini, Ameda. Reveal wealth and treasures.

17. Surya, Suryanarkoil. Bright illumination.

18. Taara, Kushalnagar. Crossing over difficulties.

19. Maandhi, Thirunallar. Dispenser of rewards.

20. Shikhi, Keezhperumpallam. Detachment attitude,

21. Shaarada, Sringeri. Grasping the essence

22. Madhumathi, Nannilam. Sweetness

23. Prathyangira, Ayyavadi. Destroyer of spells.

24. Sakra, Dharasuram. Giver of might.

25. Dandanaatha, Thanjavur. Punisher of evil.

26. Baalaa, Nemili. Liveliness of youth

27. Maariamman, Punnainallur. Transformation and change Chhinnamasta

28. Aarya, Aryankavu. Noble goodness.

29. Kamakhya, Devipuram. Cosmic womb

30. Gomathi, Sankarankovil. Activation of truth.

31. Raama, Vaduvur. Enjoyment of devotion.

32. Subrahmanya, Thiruchendur. Experience of Self.

33. Maaruthi, Sucheendram. Purification of vital breath.

34. Aghora, Thiruvenkadu. Fearlessness

35. Viraatpurusha, Chennai Kalikambal. Expansion of identity.

36. Hamsini, Chidambaram. Separation of worthy and worthless.

37. Lalitha, Thirumeeyachur. Playfulness.

38. Rudra, Kudanthai Keezhkottam. Gives forms to ideas.

39. Annapoorni, Varanasi. Nutrition to completeness.

40. Meenakshi, Madurai. Nonstop activity.

41. Naagaraja, Nagercoil. Sensitivity to surroundings,

42. Krishna, Vrindavan. Sowing seeds of love.

43. Sowmya, Thiruvenkadu. Grace.

44. Vitthala, Udupi. Steadfastness.

45. Kaali, Visakhapatnam. Power of evolution and time.

46. Yama, Srivanchiyam. Restraint of mind.

47. Parashurama, Thiruvallam. Severs bondages.

48. Paramapadam, Badrinath. Supreme state of existence.

49. Rakshasa, Thrissur. Protector of weak.

50. Chitragupta, Thirukodikaval. Accountant of deeds.

51. Shiva, Kedarnath. Eternal blessings and welfare.

52. Shurpasana, Thirunageswaram. Cleansing of desires.

53. Mahamaaya, Haridwar. Clearing of illusion.

54. Jwaala, Thiruvalanchuzhi. Spark of enlightenment.

55. Kaalasankarshini, Kanchipuram. Destruction and decay over time.

56. Kaalakaala, Thirukkadayur. Transcender of death.

57. Mookambika, Thiruvidaimarudhur. Paralyse enemy speech Bagalamukhi.

58. Vethaali, Attukal. Controller of astral spirits.

59. Muthappan, Kallar muthappanmala. Changing course of nature Vishnumaya.

60. Vanadevata, Chathuragiri. Protection from nature.

61. Guhyeshwari, Thirupurambiyam. Hides vitals from wrong hands.

62. Bhavaani, Annanagar Periyapalayathamman. Power of manifestation

63. Hethai, Nilgiri Nanjanad. Purity and Chastity.

64. Bhuvaneshwari, Pudukottai. Regulation of desire and anger.

CHAPTER FOUR

Sri Vidya

TRAILOKYAMOHANA CHAKRA

1. Brahma, Anima. Creative Energy

2. Nataraaja, Laghima. Cosmic rhythm.

3. Singaara Velan, Mahima. Upholder of love and passion.

4. Ananthashayana, Eeshithva. Aim towards infinite.

5. Vaarahi, Vashitva. Excellence in effort.

6. Indra, Prakamya. Heightened sensitivity.

7. Chamunda, Bhukti. Destroyer of ignorance.

8. Mahalakshmi, Iccha. Attainment of wealth.

9. Chakraratha, Praapti. Cyclic order of universe.

10. Sarpa, Sarvakama Siddhi. Regulation of reactive brain.

SARVAASHAPARIPOORAKA CHAKRA

1. Manmatha, Kamakarshini. Love and romance

2. Buddha, Buddhyakarshini. Enlightenment.

3. Periyanayaki, Ahankarakarshini. Giver of self confidence

4. Raajamaatangi, Shabdakarshini. Power of expounding

5. Vaayu, Sparshakarshini. Scatters ideas around

6. Vishwakarma, Rupakarshini. Activity of universe

7. Bhikshatana, Rasakarshini. Receiver of blessings

8. Praana Shakti, Gandhakarshini. Force of vital breath

9. Dakshinamurthi, Chittakarshini. Dexterity

10. Veerabhadra, Dhairyakarshini. Courage and valour.

11. Budha, Smrityakarshini. Intellectual Stimulation.

12. Akshara, Naamakarshini. Long lasting without decay

13. Nirruthi, Beejakarshini. Chaotic structure.

14. Nirgunam, Atmakarshini. Self beyond form.

15. Varuna, Amrithakarshini. Clarity of water.

16. Karuppaswami, Shareerakarshini. Protector of Dharma.

SARVASAMKSHOBHANA CHAKRA

1. Poonkurathi, Anangakusuma. Softness like a flower

2. Dharmaraja, Anangamekhala. Maintainer of righteousness.

3. Kathayi, Anangamadana. Protects from desires.

4. Rathi, Anangamadanaatura. Arousal through perception.

5. Vriddhamba, Anangarekha. Maturity and experience.

6. Garuda, Anangavegini. Remover of toxicity.

7. Visalakshi, Anangaankusha. Enhanced perception.

8. Ucchishtesha, Anangamaalini. Discarding worthless as vomit.

SARVASAUBHAGYADAYAKA CHAKRA

1. Shoolini, sarvasamkshobhini. Destroyer of Trigunas

2. Kathavaraya, sarvavidravini. Clarity of vision Sudarshana

3. Raahu, sarvakarshini. Exposes and Cleans temptations.

4. Neela, sarvahladini. Pleasure and joy

5. Mohini, sarvasammohini. Fascinator of people Kurukulla

6. Pechi, sarvasthambhini. Prevents mishappenings

7. Ashvarudha, sarvajrumbhini. Creates and reserve sankalpas in future

8. Yogeshwari, sarvavashankari. Alignment of body mind soul

9. Chandra, sarvaranjini. Cool and composure

10. Kethu, sarvonmadini. Progress spiritually

11. Shankaranarayani, sarvarthasadhini. Guides towards well being

12. Kubera, sarvasampattipurani. Blessing of abundance

13. Gaayathri, sarvamantramayi. Stimulation of consciousness

14. Aaditya, sarvadvandvakshayankari. Breaks limitations

SARVAARTHASADHAKA CHAKRA

1. Siddhishwara, sarvasiddhiprada. Giver of accomplishment

2. Brihaspathi, sarvasampatprada. Expansion of presence

3. Govinda, sarvapriyankari. Attractor of devotion.

4. Mangala, sarvamangalakarini. Auspiciousness without deficiency

5. Kaamadhenu, sarvakamaprada. Fulfillment of desires.

6. Jyeshta, sarvadukhavimochini. Primordial force of self.

7. Bhairava, sarvamrityuprashamani. Removes fear Tripurabhairavi

8. Ganapathi, sarvavighnanivarini. Transcends stereotyping

9. Pachaiamman, sarvaangasundari. Growth and fertility

10. Raajaraajeshwari, sarvasaubhagyadayini. Rulership.

SARVARAKSHAKARA CHAKRA

1. Saraswathi, sarvajna. Strategic knowledge

2. Anjaneya, sarvashakti. Superpower of vision

3. Prithvi, sarvaishwaryaprada. Giver of prosperity

4. Hayagriva, sarvajnanamayi. Clarity of mind and intellect

5. Jwarahara, sarvavyadhinivarini. Healer of disease and ailment

6. Muneeshwara, sarvadharaswarupa. Eloquence of silence

7. Chandika, sarvapapahara. Ferocious against evil.

8. Nandi, sarvanandamayi. Peace and stillness

9. Durga, sarvarakshaswarupini. Protect like a fortress

10. Shanishwara, sarvepsitaphalaprada. Endurance and forbearance

SARVAROGAHARA CHAKRA

1. Saastha, vashini. Governance of divine

2. Kamakshi, kaameshi. Rule by regulating desires

3. Shukra, modini. Enjoyment

4. Kamalalayam, vimala. Dissolve everything in self

5. Agni, aruna. Burning all negativity

6. Narasimha, jayini. Animistic raw power and might

7. Sharabha, sarveshi. Power of destruction

8. Maanasa, kaulini. Control of mind.

SARVASIDDHIPRADA CHAKRA

1. Sheethala, kameshwari. Showers of blessings

2. Renuka, vajreshwari. Indestructible strength

3. Angaalamman, bhagamalini. Primordial vibration Omkara.

4. Champa, thureeya. Support from nature Chempazhanthy

SARVANANDAMAYA CHAKRA

1. Thyaagaraja, Sadashiva Mancha. Rulership through sacrifice.

2. Parabhattarika, Maha Tripurasundari. The most transcendental.

Kaama Sevitha

1. Sumeru. Eternal honeymoon heaven of Atma Amma marriage.

2. Vaalai. Intense romantic consort of Kalki in marriage Venkateshwara form.

The Peak of Mount Sumeru

Vaalai

Maha Samrajya Shalini

Maha Samrajya Shalini

OORDHVA LOKAS

1. Bhoolokam. Lamenting, speculating and criticizing about the past results in making you nirgathi without solace.

2. Bhuvarlokam. Seeking pleasure in worldly things only gives scorched heat and stunted shadeless trees.

3. Swarlokam. Ahankara and ego leads o death, misery, devastation and famine.

4. Maharlokam. Recognizing self greatness and seekin all pleasures without dependency on others rewarded with sought enjoyment as well as external pleasures too.

5. Janalokam. Excess procreation leads to Matsya Nyaya where power is captured by hook or crook.

6. Thapalokam. Tapas, mantras aimed at fixed objectives leads to usage of astras causing social changes, pandemics and so on.

7. Sathyalokam. Catching hold on to promises, truth and words spoken leads to disruption in communications.

ADHARA LOKAS

1. Athalam. Lies and distorting of truth leads to abandonment and humiliation

2. Vithalam. Disturbing of others lives leads to distress caused from one's own beloved ones and kids.

3. Suthalam. Lust and interest in physical bodily pleasure leads into exposing of privacy

4. Thalaathalam. Dissatisfaction with divine will leads to instability and roaming.

5. Rasathalam. Emotional instability leads to loss of wealth, loved ones and property.

6. Mahaathalam. Seeking of greatness and devotion rewarded with access to divine realms.

7. Paathaalam. Trying to hack and influence the Divine and sinning leads to violence and cruel painful death.

SAMASHTI ROOPAM

1. Kalki. The Vishwarupam with five components of Sri Shodashakshari Vidya, as explained earlier.

2. Atma. The life of Kalki, which is myself.

Kalki with the fourteen Lokas